20 FUN FACTS ABOUT ELECTRICITY

BY KATIE KAWA

Gareth Stevens PUBLISHING

Please visit our website, www.garethstevens.com. For a free color catalog of all our high-quality books, call toll free 1-800-542-2595 or fax 1-877-542-2596.

Cataloging-in-Publication Data
Names: Kawa, Katie.
Title: 20 fun facts about electricity / Katie Kawa.
Description: New York : Gareth Stevens Publishing, 2024. | Series: Fun fact file: inventions that changed the world | Includes glossary and index.
Identifiers: ISBN 9781538287613 (pbk.) | ISBN 9781538287620 (library bound) | ISBN 9781538287637 (ebook)
Subjects: LCSH: Electricity–Juvenile literature. | Electricity–History–Juvenile literature.
Classification: LCC QC527.2 K39 2024 | DDC 537–dc23

First Edition

Published in 2024 by
Gareth Stevens Publishing
2544 Clinton Street
Buffalo, NY 14224

Designer: Leslie Taylor
Editor: Therese Shea

Photo credits: Cover (main) TWStock/Shutterstock.com; file folder used throughout David Smart/Shutterstock.com; binder clip used throughout luckyraccoon/Shutterstock.com; wood grain background used throughout ARENA Creative/Shutterstock.com; p. 4 (lightning) d1sk/Shutterstock.com, (vintage bulbs) Champiofoto/Shutterstock.com; p. 5 Alhovik/Shutterstock.com; p. 6 Digital Genetics/Shutterstock.com; p. 7 MikeRun/https://commons.wikimedia.org/wiki/File:Attractive-electric-force-between-hair-and-balloon.jpg; p. 8 (inset) J J Osuna Caballero/Shutterstock.com, (Baghdad) Rasool Ali/Shutterstock.com; p. 9 haryigit/Shutterstock.com; p. 10 https://commons.wikimedia.org/wiki/File:Benjamin West, English (born America) - Benjamin Franklin Drawing Electricity from the Sky - Google Art Project.jpg; p. 11 Everett Collection/Shutterstock.com; p. 12 https://en.wikipedia.org/wiki/File:Light_bulb_Edison_2.jpg; p. 13 BijanStock/Shutterstock.com; p. 14 rady-Handy Photograph Collection/https://en.wikipedia.org/wiki/File:Edison_and_phonograph_edit1.jpg; p. 15 Helen89/Shutterstock.com; p. 16 https://commons.wikimedia.org/wiki/File:Tesla_circa_1890.jpeg; p. 17 Dickenson V. Alley/https://en.wikipedia.org/wiki/File:Nikola_Tesla,_with_his_equipment_Wellcome_M0014782_-_restoration2.jpg; p. 18 Yuliasis/Shutterstock.com; p. 19 peterschreiber.media/Shutterstock.com; p. 20 https://commons.wikimedia.org/wiki/File:Thomas_Parker_Electric_car.jpg; p. 21 canadianPhotographer56/Shutterstock.com; p. 22 Rudmer Zwerver/Shutterstock.com; p. 23 BlueRingMedia/Shutterstock.com; p. 24 smereka/Shutterstock.com; p. 25 matimix/Shutterstock.com; p. 26 ABCDstock/Shutterstock.com; p. 27 Sebastian Noethlichs/Shutterstock.com; p. 29 MintImages/Shutterstock.com.

Printed in the United States of America

CONTENTS

Words in the glossary appear in **bold** type the first time they are used in the text.

IT'S ELECTRIC!

Electricity powers inventions we use every day—from light bulbs to computers. It helps us cook, clean, keep warm, and so much more. It's also found in nature in lightning, some animals, and even the human body!

So what exactly is electricity? It's the flow of some of the tiniest parts of matter—called electrons—from one place to another. Keep reading to find out how people learned to control this flow to create the electric world we know today.

Atom Structure

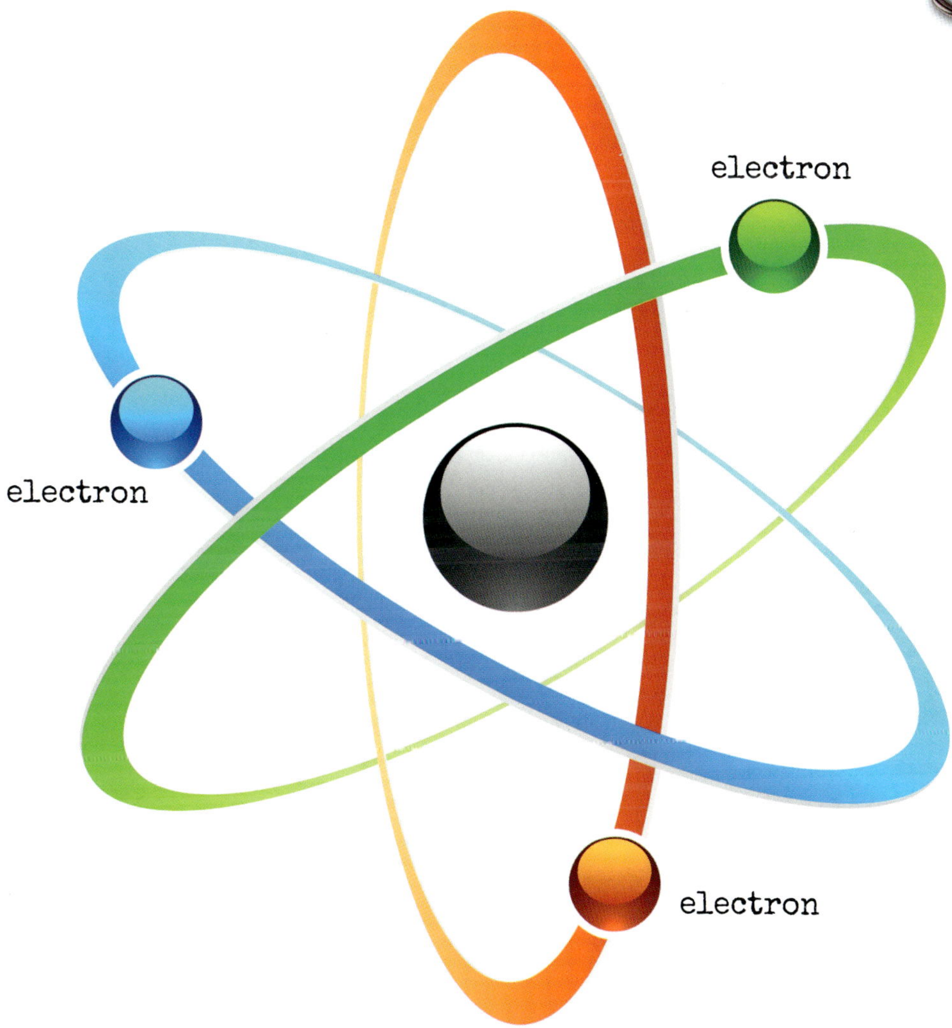

Atoms are the building blocks of all matter. Even smaller **particles** make up atoms. An atom model is shown here. Electricity is the movement of electrons between atoms.

EARLY ELECTRICITY EXPERIMENTS

FUN FACT: 1

NO ONE INVENTED ELECTRICITY!

People have invented many kinds of machines that use electricity to make our lives easier.

Electricity is a part of nature, so no one invented it. We're also not sure who first discovered that it could be used as a kind of power. Many people experimented with electricity, invented ways to **generate** it, and created machines that use it.

If you've ever rubbed a balloon on your head and then watched your hair stand up, you've experimented with static electricity!

FUN FACT: 2

THE ANCIENT GREEKS KNEW ABOUT ELECTRICITY.

Electricity isn't a modern discovery. Greeks experimented with static electricity around 600 BCE. Static electricity is an electric charge, or kind of electricity, that builds up when two things are rubbed together.

THE BEGINNING OF BATTERIES

FUN FACT: 3

A 2,000-YEAR-OLD OBJECT FOUND IN BAGHDAD, IRAQ, MAY BE AN ANCIENT BATTERY.

Scientists found a clay jar, iron rod, and copper tube in the 1930s. Together, they could have been used as a battery, though scientists aren't sure they were. Scientists named it the Baghdad Battery.

Batteries use **chemicals** to generate electricity. The Baghdad Battery can generate a small amount of electricity when filled with vinegar, for example.

Baghdad

the Baghdad Battery

FUN FACT: 4

BATTERIES CAN BE MADE WITH SALT WATER, PICKLES, AND POTATOES.

The idea behind Volta's battery, called the voltaic pile, can be seen in experiments that use potatoes to generate electricity.

Electricity can travel through salt water, as well as many fruits and vegetables. An early battery made in 1800 by Alessandro Volta used cloth or cardboard soaked in salt water placed between different metals.

FRANKLIN'S SHOCKING EXPERIMENT

FUN FACT: 5

ONE OF THE FOUNDIING FATHERS OF THE UNITED STATES EXPERIMENTED WITH ELECTRICITY.

Benjamin Franklin played a big part in the early history of the United States. He was also a scientist. He came up with a plan to capture electricity from lightning using a kite and a metal key.

Franklin's kite experiment likely took place in 1752. He said he felt a shock from the electricity!

Franklin probably stayed under a roof or inside during the lightning storm to stay safe. Pictures like this one don't show the true story.

FUN FACT: 6

FRANKLIN'S EXPERIMENT COULD HAVE BEEN DEADLY.

Franklin most likely felt a shock from electricity in the air, not from lightning. A lightning strike would have killed him! In fact, another scientist was killed in 1753 trying Franklin's experiment.

A GREAT INVENTOR

FUN FACT: 7

THOMAS EDISON INVENTED MANY THINGS—BUT NOT THE LIGHT BULB.

Many people think Edison was the inventor of the light bulb. But inventors were working with light bulbs before he was born! Edison created a better light bulb around 1880 that made electric lighting popular.

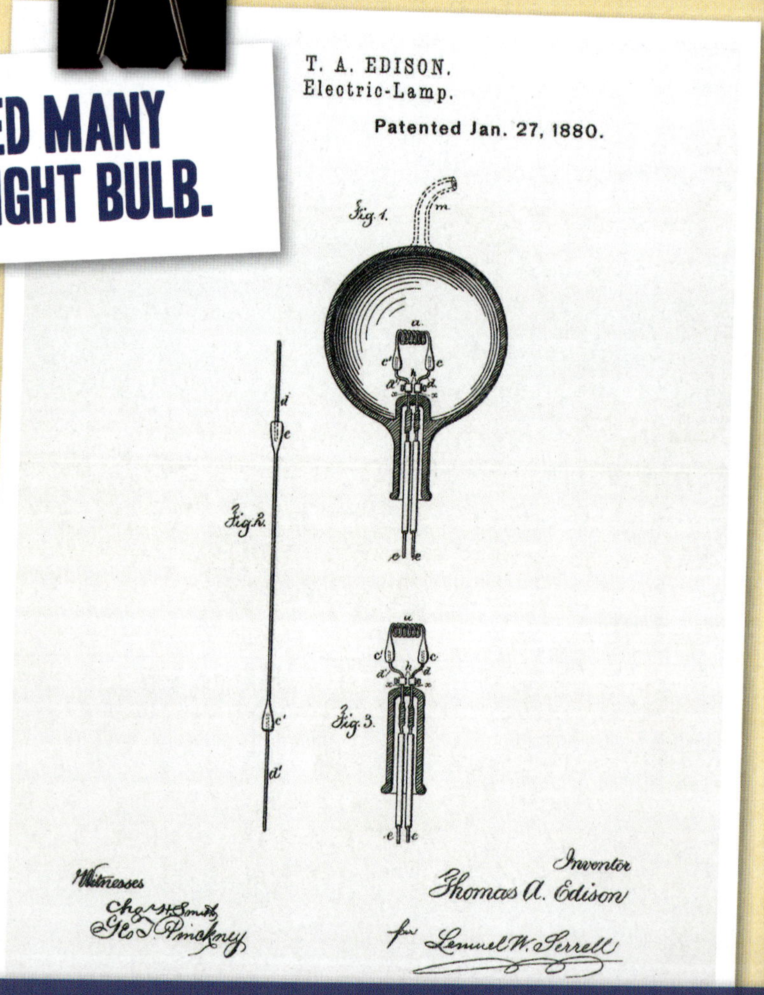

Edison went to school for only a few years. At that time, it was common for children to stop going to school early in life.

PARTS OF AN ELECTRIC CIRCUIT

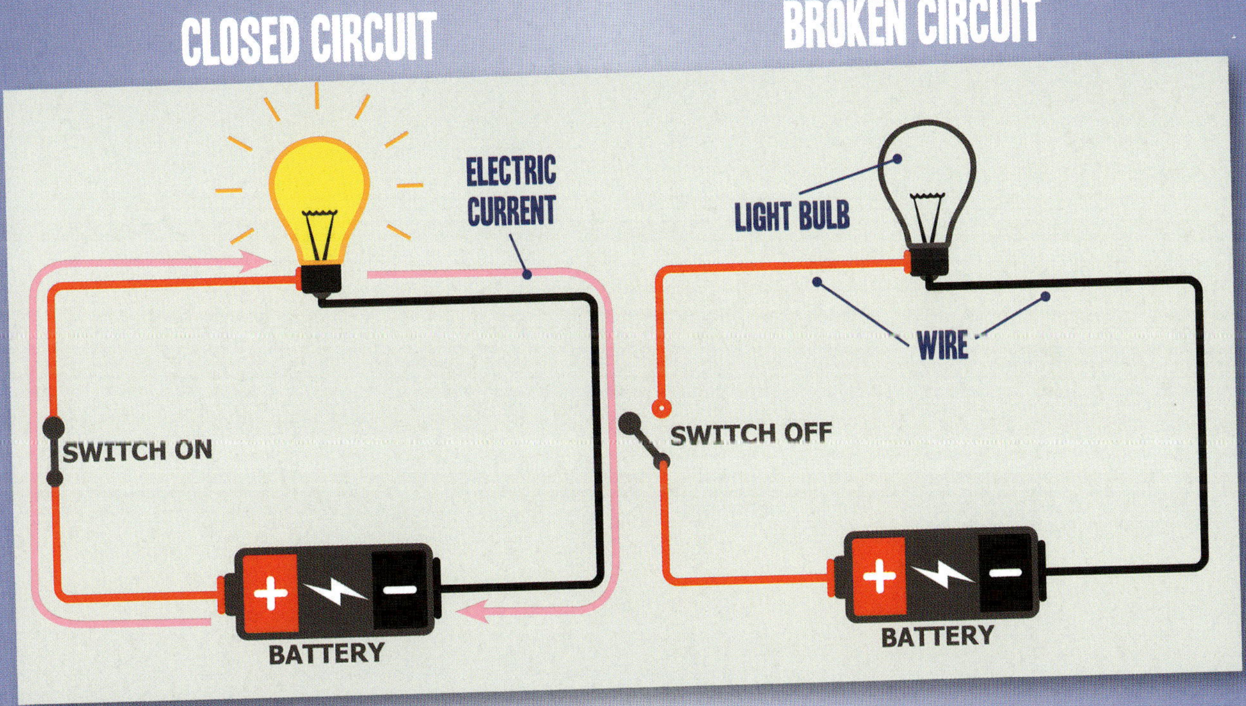

Light bulbs are part of an electric circuit. Flipping a **switch** can break the circuit, which stops the flow of electricity and turns off the light. In a closed circuit, electricity flows, and the bulb lights up.

FUN FACT: 8

THOMAS EDISON HELD MORE THAN 1,000 U.S. PATENTS BY THE TIME HE DIED.

A patent is a government statement that says others can't use your idea or make your product. Edison's many patents had to do with electrical inventions, including **phonographs**, lights, telephones, and batteries.

Edison is pictured here in 1878 with his phonograph. Some called him a wizard for making this invention!

Edison had many successes and failures in his lab, which is shown here. He once said, "I have not failed 10,000 times—I've successfully found 10,000 ways that will not work."

FUN FACT: 9

THOMAS EDISON FAILED THOUSANDS OF TIMES.

Failure is an important teacher, and Edison understood this. It's said it took 3,000 tries to find what would work as the Edison light bulb's filament, which is the wire or thread that lights up.

TESLA TAKES THE SPOTLIGHT

FUN FACT: 10

THERE WAS A "WAR" OVER ELECTRICITY!

In the late 1800s, Edison **competed** with inventor Nikola Tesla in what's become known as the "war of the currents." Tesla's alternating current (AC) was better than Edison's direct current (DC) at carrying electric power a long way.

Nikola Tesla helped make AC the main kind of current used in the United States. AC is an electrical current that changes its direction over and over. DC always flows in one direction.

Tesla said he wanted his ray to be used to stop wars. However, reporters liked the name "death ray" rather than "peace beam."

FUN FACT: 11

TESLA WANTED TO INVENT A DEATH RAY!

Tesla invented many things. One that thankfully never got made was his death ray. He said he had plans for an invention that could shoot down planes using beams of electrically charged particles.

SENDING SIGNALS

FUN FACT: 12

ELECTRICITY HELPS US TALK WHEN WE'RE FAR APART.

We use electricity to charge the phones, tablets, and laptops we use to talk to each other today.

In 1844, Samuel Morse sent the first message using a telegraph. This invention carried messages using electrical **signals**. Alexander Graham Bell received a patent for the telephone in 1876. Telephones change sounds into electrical signals.

Pacemakers work because the human heart has its own kind of electrical system to control how it beats.

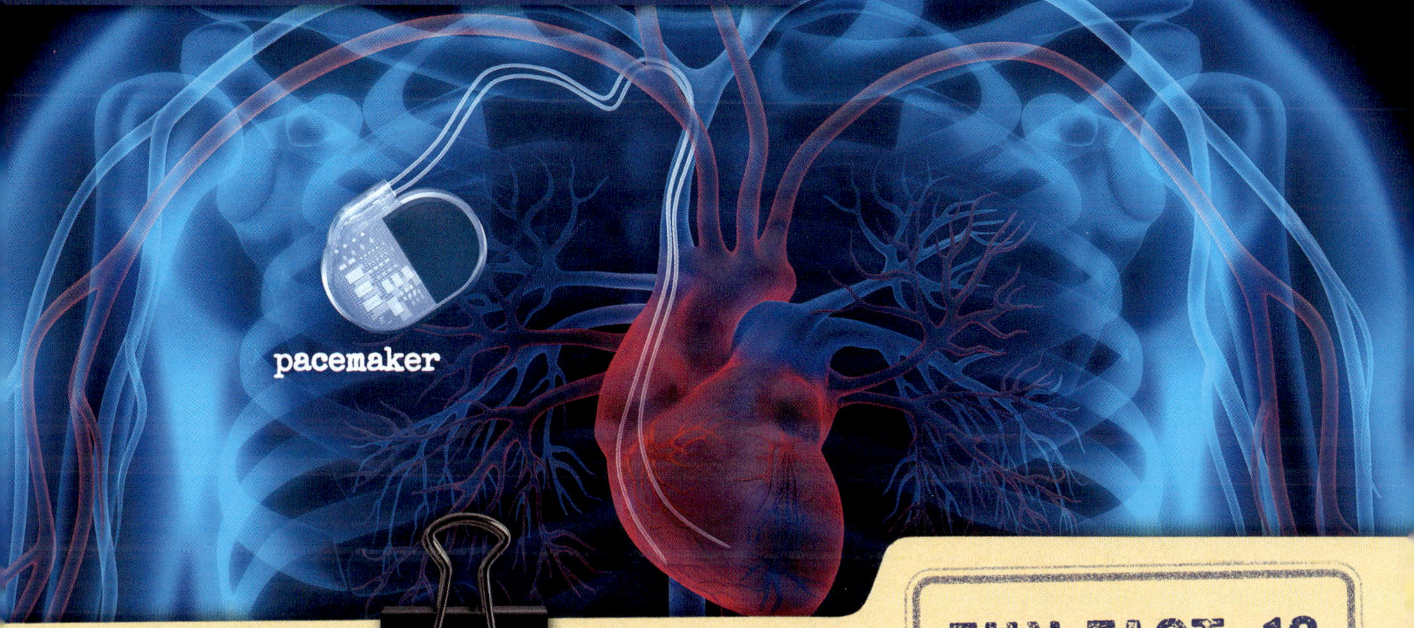

FUN FACT: 13

ELECTRICITY CAN FIX A BROKEN HEART.

Devices called pacemakers control the rhythm, or beating, of the human heart when the heart can't do that on its own. Pacemakers are placed in the chest. There, they send electrical signals to the heart to correct its beat.

ELECTRIC CARS

FUN FACT: 14

ELECTRIC CARS EXISTED 50 YEARS BEFORE CARS THAT USE GAS.

Electric cars aren't a recent invention! Cars invented in the 1830s used electric **motors**. Cars that run on gas weren't invented until years later, in the 1880s.

Electric **vehicles** (EVs), such as the one shown here, made it easier for people and goods to travel from place to place.

Electric cars are more popular—and faster—than ever. Many car companies are planning to make more EVs in the future.

FUN FACT: 15

TODAY'S ELECTRIC CARS ARE MORE THAN 18 TIMES FASTER THAN THE FIRST EVs.

In 1890, the fastest electric car in the United States reached a top speed of 14 miles (23 km) per hour. Today's fastest electric cars can go up to 258 miles (415 km) per hour!

FACTS ABOUT FOSSIL FUELS

FUN FACT: 16

PREHISTORIC PLANTS CAN PRODUCE ELECTRICITY.

Places that make electric energy, or power, are called power plants. They often use fossil fuels. Fossil fuels, such as coal, oil, and natural gas, come from plants and other things that lived millions of years ago!

This power plant uses coal to generate electricity. Fossils fuels are harmful to nature, so people are looking for cleaner ways to produce power.

HOW DOES A COAL POWER PLANT WORK?

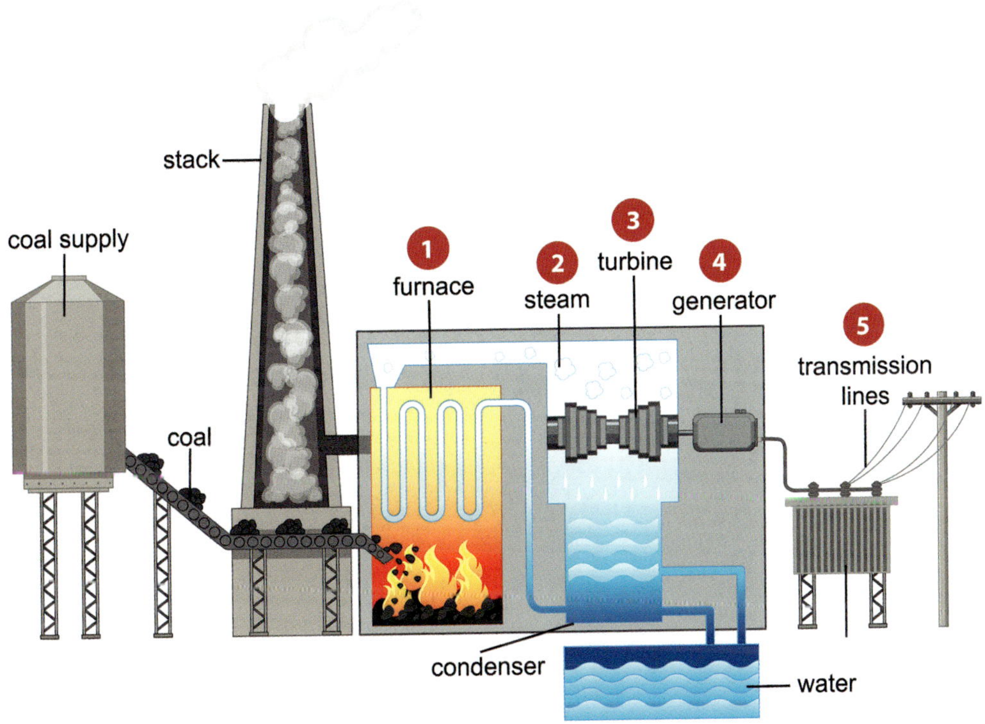

1. THE COAL IS BURNED IN THE FURNACE.
2. THE COAL HEATS THE WATER AND CREATES STEAM.
3. THE STEAM TURNS THE BLADES OF THE **TURBINE**.
4. THE GENERATOR TURNS THE POWER FROM THE MOVING BLADES INTO ELECTRICITY.
5. THE TRANSMISSION LINES, OR POWER LINES, CARRY ELECTRICITY TO HOMES AND BUSINESSES.

Generators in today's power plants are based on the ideas of inventor Michael Faraday, who invented the first generator in 1831.

NEW KINDS OF POWER

FUN FACT: 17

YOU CAN POWER YOUR HOME WITH ANIMAL POOP!

Biomass is matter from living things that can be burned to produce electricity. It includes wood and parts of plants such as corn. Manure—animal poop—is also an example of biomass.

Some farmers are turning cow poop into electric power!

The energy produced by people's movement doesn't harm nature like the energy produced by fossil fuels does.

FUN FACT: 18

SOME SOCCER FIELDS ARE LIT BY PLAYERS' ENERGY!

In 2014, a soccer field was built in Brazil in South America that turned the energy from moving feet into electricity to light the field. Another field like this was built in Nigeria in Africa in 2015.

POWER TO THE PEOPLE

FUN FACT: 19

THERE ARE ENOUGH POWER LINES IN THE UNITED STATES TO REACH THE MOON AND BACK!

In the United States, there are over 600,000 miles (965,606 km) of power lines. That's more than twice the distance between Earth and the moon, which is about 238,855 miles (384,400 km).

Power lines carry electricity from power plants to homes and businesses.

Some areas of Africa are without electricity. Africa is one of the best places to make solar energy. Solar cells, devices that change sunlight into electricity, are shown here.

FUN FACT: 20

MORE PEOPLE ARE ABLE TO USE ELECTRICITY THAN EVER BEFORE.

As of 2021, about 90 percent of the world had access to electricity. This means they were able to get and use it. Groups that help people around the world hope that number grows.

A BRIGHT FUTURE

Inventors such as Benjamin Franklin, Thomas Edison, and Nikola Tesla shaped the history of electricity. They took power that came from nature and found ways to get it and use it to change the world.

Today, people are looking for ways to use fewer fossil fuels and generate more electricity using renewable resources. Renewable resources are power sources that won't run out. They include water, wind, and the sun. Maybe you'll come up with your own invention to shape the future of electricity!

The future of electricity looks bright!

GLOSSARY

chemical: Matter that can be mixed with other matter to cause changes.

compete: To try to win a contest with others.

device: A tool or machine made to perform a task.

Founding Father: A man who had a role in forming the U.S. government.

generate: To produce something or cause something to be produced.

motor: A machine that produces motion or power for doing work.

particle: A very small piece of something.

phonograph: A device used to play music records, also called a record player.

prehistoric: Having to do with the time before written history.

signal: An electric current that sends a message. Also, the message sent using electronic communication.

switch: A device that opens, closes, or changes the connections in an electrical circuit.

turbine: A motor operated by the movement of water, steam, or air.

vehicle: An object used for carrying or transporting people or goods, such as a car, truck, or airplane.

FOR MORE INFORMATION

BOOKS

Amson-Bradshaw, Georgia. *Electricity*. New York, NY: PowerKids Press, 2020.

Dickmann, Nancy. *Lewis Latimer: The Man Behind a Better Light Bulb*. North Mankato, MN: Pebble, 2020.

Midthun, Joseph. *Electricity*. Chicago, IL: World Book, 2022.

WEBSITES

Be a Power Saver
climatekids.nasa.gov/power-savers/
This NASA website explains problems with fossil fuels and the importance of renewable resources.

Electricity
www.dkfindout.com/us/science/electricity/
Explore different areas of electricity—from batteries and circuits to static electricity and electric animals.

Thomas Edison for Kids
www.nps.gov/edis/learn/kidsyouth/index.htm
The Thomas Edison National Historic Park website educates about the man behind the light bulb and other inventions.

INDEX